Relentless Mode

– DIANA MUGANO –

An environmentally friendly book printed and bound in England by
www.printondemand-worldwide.com

This book is made entirely of chain-of-custody materials

www.fast-print.net/store.php

Relentless Mode

A catalogue record for this book is available from the British Library

ISBN 978-178456-000-3

First published 2014 by
FASTPRINT PUBLISHING
Peterborough, England.

Contents

Dedication

I dedicate this book to my heavenly father, creator of heaven and earth, to my wonderful mother who taught me to be humble all the time, to my daddy who taught me to be thankful all the time, to my lovely sister Margret Mugano – I appreciate you a lot – to my baby brothers Tatenda and Tawanda Mugano – I salute you both. I am also giving a shout to those who are going through the following: failure, pain, frustration, delay, hardship, struggle, refusal, humiliation, disappointment, ugly situations, rejection, hurt, if you've had enough or any bad name that I have not mentioned that causes you to lose your joy. I say it's not over until you declare it's over yourself. Never quit!

Preface

I was thinking of writing a book… but so many topics came into my mind. Above all the topics there was one that kept coming back: this one rich word… relentless. I looked at many successful people in life and concluded that they were all very relentless and after I found this out I made a journey to many bookshops to see if they were books written on this topic: I started thinking of how to write it, resource it and publish it. One day on a journey back from work when I was tired, fed up, hungry, broke, frustrated, waiting on a platform on a very cold winter day and just needed comfort, so many things came in my mind and I started thinking again how to write this book. This book is written to encourage that person who wants to give up.

I was strongly moved to write this book because I went on such a journey called life and no one can predict what tomorrow holds… but only if you don't quit on your vision early and be relentless then you will surely overcome.

Here is my sevenfold goal of writing this book:

- I want you to be encouraged.
- You are not alone in this journey called life.
- Quitting is not an option.
- I want to give you some principles to help you understand when a situation arises.
- I want you to understand what to do when you find yourself in a situation.
- I want you to understand that there is a solution for every situation.
- Life always offers you a second chance - it's called tomorrow.

When all these components come together victory shall be yours. As you read this book I believe you are going to find some nuggets that will help you approach life in a positive manner.

If you have a goal, be relentless in your pursuit (Keith J Davis Jr).

History is a relentless master. It has no present, only the past rushing into the future. To try to hold fast is to be swept aside (John F Kennedy).

On every side, and at every hour of the day, we came up against the relentless limitations of pioneer life (Anna H Shaw).

You must be passionate, you must dedicate yourself, and you must be relentless in the pursuit of your goals. If you do you will be successful.

(Steve Garvey).

There have been so many people who have said to me, 'You can't do that,' but I've had an innate belief that they were wrong. Be unwavering and relentless in your approach.

(Halle Berry).

Introduction

At some point in one's life a situation will occur which is unpleasant: some are made by us and some are of unknown origin. Now that these situations have occurred it does not mean that you have to give up on life.

This book is written to encourage anyone who is on the verge of giving up. Its title is Relentless Mode: I came up with this title after experiencing the ups and downs of what I call life. On a very cold day waiting for a train I just started thinking how Thomas Edison came up with the idea of the electric light bulb and remembered reading his biography: he failed 10,000 times and despite all these challenges he never gave up on his dream.

I'm sure through this transition Thomas Edison must have thought of giving up at some point but he had a **turning point**, **struggled**, had an **experience** and had numerous **opportunities** to do it again. He had to

embrace failure through the process: he must have felt as if he were an **unsuccessful person,** then he made up his mind that he was going to be **consistent**, had a **second chance** and at the end of it all he became a **successful person**. All these principles will - I believe - help anyone to be relentless and achieve their goals.

I have applied all these principles in each chapter. They might be used together - or you can choose one that applies to your situation and apply it to achieve your aim in life. There is nothing in life that gets our attention as much as an unpleasant situation and it's at this point that change is paramount. Some people will not accept change because of fear, pride, laziness, lack of knowledge - or they may be unable to recognise the need for change. They may be procrastinators, it may go against their belief system or it might serve a different purpose in their life.

It is at this moment that you have to make a decision and remain relentless. Relentless means yielding to compassion. When you are relentless about something you mean business: you do not stop until you get what you want. The principles written in this book will help you solve that challenge or that problem you are facing: I have put tips with each principle and I believe they will serve you well.

First Chapter

Consistency

To be a consistent winner means preparing not just one day, one month or even one year, but for a lifetime (Bill Rodgers).

You always really have to remain consistent in your beliefs and philosophy (Mark Messier).

In essence, if we want to direct our lives we must take control of our consistent actions. It's not what we do once in a while that shapes our lives, but what we do consistently (Tony Robbins).

The word consistent means: of a regularly occurring, dependable nature. One might say: he/she is very consistent in his/her performance, week in week out; he/she always scores good goals. Personality in humans can be defined as the characteristics of individuals which describe and account for consistent patterns of feeling, thinking and behaving.

HOW TO BECOME A CONSISTENT WINNER

Goals are essential in becoming a consistent winner. Goals have been written about in more books than can be counted, but even with all these missives written about goals this resource is underused.

A goal is where you want to end up in any particular endeavour. It is the result that you seek and the outcome that you desire. In this regard some think that goals are only to be identified when you want something important or large. However, setting and reaching goals is a skill and - like anything else - requires skill. You have got to practice skills. The consistent targeting and hitting of small goals is like taking consistent small steps. If you keep going you will reach any destination.

You might have a negative reaction to having so many goals but if you take a look at the people who are the most productive and happy they will tell you that they live their life by design, not by default. You need to be aware of your thoughts, emotions and actions. Being self-aware and living by design means that you are intentional about the results and the outcomes in your life. Remain focused on what matters most in what you are doing and why you are doing it.

TIPS

1. Write your goals down: that's a good place to start. In this manner you articulate them. Writing involves the physical use of pen and paper along with seeing it and reading it: your

brain has a more powerful and supportive relationship to the sight of it written out. In addition, you are giving instructions to your subconscious every time you read it.

2. It's important to identify the goals that you want, not the goals you don't want. In this way you are moving towards what you want rather than away from what you don't want.
3. You'll want to be positive in how you construct your goals. It's important to use only affirmative words: avoid using words like not, never and don't.
4. Be grateful in the expectation of achieving your goals.
5. Use emotionally-charged adjectives to express your goals.
6. Be as specific as possible. Your mind likes details and it is especially powerful to your planning process to have your goal particulars acknowledged.
7. The goal works best when it is tied to a purpose or to a compelling reason for why you want it. The purpose adds its own energy to the process and can catapult you into achieving it.
8. You'll want it to be measurable so that you will know when you have achieved it - and for aiming purposes the feedback of hitting the mark is empowering.

9. The goal must be achievable.
10. Having time-bound goals is also a powerful point. Putting your goals in a realistic time frame really helps the subconscious accept that this is a matter-of-fact endeavour.

HOW TO TAKE CONTROL OF OUR CONSISTENT ACTIONS

In most cases the biggest challenge is making consistent actions. Consistency is not the most exciting word but if it is coupled with time it will give real results in your life. Personally, some days go well; some days really don't: sticking with your belief and doing something consistently and not just when you feel inspired is awesome. To become consistent in many areas is great but you have to remember that variation and setbacks are stimulating and valuable parts of life. But still, improvements can be made.

TIPS

Morning rituals.

Here is my typical example, which I normally follow. You simply set up a routine in the morning that you do as soon as you wake up. This works so well because what you do early in the day often sets the context for your day. As humans we have a strong tendency to want to be consistent with what we have done before. That's one big reason why a bad start often leads to a bad day and a good start often leads to a good day.

I like this morning ritual:

- Read Bible.
- Get up; drink glass of water.
- Pull curtains/blinds from windows and let fresh air in.
- Eat breakfast and drink cup of green tea.
- Brush teeth and tongue.
- Make bed.
- Declutter for few minutes. Wash remaining dishes from last night. Put anything that is out of place into its right place.

Basically, this will help you to get organised and have a productive mindset by doing these simple things to order and clean up your environment. It is also a good way to warm up for your day and get out of a procrastinating way of thinking.

1. Do things even if you don't feel like it.

Your inner voice and feelings can be disregarded if you like… just doing it is still not always easy to pull off. But I have found a few insights that make it a whole lot easier.

Eckhart Tolle says, 'You are not your thoughts. I have realised that I am not really my thoughts. I'm the one observing my thoughts. The thoughts are something that moves through my mind. You are not your emotions: not listening to your thoughts too much gets easier after a while. It can be harder not to listen to your emotions. This is not to say that your thoughts or emotions are worthless, but sometimes you can tell when they are mostly just holding you back. And if you are less identified with them and less wrapped up in them it becomes easier to act in spite of what they are suggesting that you should do.

This can be helpful if you want to establish a new habit. You will improve faster and stick to your new habit until it sticks to you (if you don't fold quickly) as your mind gets over the initial enthusiasm and starts to invent reasons for you to give up - and the great thing is it's kind of liberating. You realise that you don't have to obey or act in accordance with your thought loops or emotions.

2. Don't hurt yourself.

Realise that when you disappoint yourself and don't think and do as you really want to that you hurt yourself by lowering your self-esteem. Whatever you do during your day sends signals back to you about what kind of person you are. Do the right thing - like being effective or kind.

3. Focus on and take responsibility for the process, not the potential results.

Focus on the process and you will be a lot more relaxed and inclined to continue than if you stare yourself blind on the potential results that never come as quickly as you want to. Not focusing puts you on an emotional roller coaster from day to day.

4. Find and do what you love or like to do.

It's always easier to stick with the stuff you love - or at least like - what you are doing every week. So experiment and find what suits you best.

5. Use reminders in your environment.

Write down what you really want to make into a habit or a natural part of your life on a Post-it note or on the screen saver of your computer.

6. Let go of old self-images.

How you dress can affect how you feel and how you see yourself, so you may want to take a look at what you wear and what your shoes, shirt, dress, skirt etc tell you and how they make you feel. And then think about how a change in how you dress could help you change your thoughts and behaviour. Imagine how you will dress in the future, when you have reached your goals.

CONSISTENCY IS OUR CHOICE

If you consistently make good choices then you will more than likely be successful in all your endeavours. Many of us have to make decisions that define who we are and what we believe in. Most often the choices we face may seem insignificant but this doesn't mean that they are not important to us. Even the smallest action can have an impact on our self-respect and our integrity.

There are so many benefits when we choose consistency as our choice in life: first, living life with consistency means that we never have to spend time or energy questioning ourselves. When we listen to our hearts and do the right thing life becomes simple. Second, we become dependable and accountable for our actions.

TIPS

1. Define the values of consistency.

You can't live by values if you don't know what you truly believe in. So start by defining your consistent values. These are the values that, no matter what the consequence, you are not going to compromise on.

2. Analyse every choice you make.

You will usually know what's right and wrong, although sometimes you might need some quiet time to figure it out.

3. Encourage consistency.

Work on building and improving consistency within yourself, so that you have the strength and courage to do the right thing when the time comes. Build your self-confidence and self-esteem and work on developing your character. Spend time getting to know yourself and what you believe in.

4. Never tell yourself 'I'm not motivated.'

That's not the real problem, unless you really don't want to make a consistent choice.

5. Build momentum one step at a time.

It's never easy to change old habits or start new routines. Studies show that it takes anything from 21 to 40 days to really turn a new behaviour into a consistent habit and, during that time, you are going to have to work at it diligently even when you don't feel like it. The key to long consistency is building momentum.

I believe that life is constantly testing us for our level of commitment and that life's greatest rewards are reserved for those who demonstrate a never-ending commitment to act until they achieve. This level of resolve can move mountains, but it must be constant and consistent. As simplistic as this may sound, it is still the common denominator separating those who live their dreams from those who live in regret.

(Tony Robbins).

Second Chapter

Experience

Experience is one thing you can't get for nothing - (Oscar Wilde).

Experience is a good school. But the fees are high - (Heinrich Heine).

Experience is simply the name we give our mistakes - (Oscar Wilde).

Experience is the only prophecy of wise men - (Alphonse de Lamartine).

If we could sell our experiences for what they cost us, we'd all be millionaires - (Pauline Phillips).

I think we are a product of all our experiences - (Sanford I. Weill).

Nothing ever becomes real till it is experienced - (John Keats).

You cannot create experience. You must undergo it - (Albert Camus).

People grow through experience if they meet life honestly and courageously. This is how character is built - (Eleanor Roosevelt).

According to The Oxford English Dictionary experience denotes knowledge of or skill of something or some event, gained through involvement in or exposure to that thing or event. An experience can be thought of as the fact of being consciously the subject of a state or condition, or of being consciously affected by an event. The concept of experience generally refers to know-how or procedural knowledge and has been a subject of interest in philosophy.

EXPERIENCE IS A GOOD SCHOOL

One of the greatest things you can do for yourself is to learn from every single experience you have ever had. Each and every day you have experiences and you choose what to do with them. The wisest people are the ones who see every experience as an opportunity to learn. Smart people can transform even the smallest experiences into the lessons that drive them to become better at everything they undertake in the future. You, too, can learn from your experiences and - in so doing - benefit tremendously.

In every experience there are things that did and did not work for you. Your objective is to learn from what happened. The more you learn from your experiences the more effective you will be at whatever you do in your life.

Life is another name for ups and downs. All of us learn new things throughout our lives and the learning phase never ends. In my opinion the best way of learning about life is through personal experience. Some people, on the contrary, believe that we can learn about life by listening to the advice of family and friends. We learn by our past experiences, which help us in making the right decisions. The end result of our actions always leaves a strong impact on our mind. On the other hand, if we listen to the advice of our family and friends we will remember that advice for a short duration only and after that we will forget their advice to us.

The advice of our family and friends is also very beneficial. Our parents are older than us and hence more experienced. They can guide us from their experiences and make suggestions to us how to move in the right direction.

To sum up, although we learn from our family and friends the best way of learning is through our experiences. This is because our experiences teach us a lesson and help us learn from our mistakes.

TIPS

1. The best way to learn from your experiences.

Learning from your experiences is one of the ways in which we decide to cultivate more of what we like about ourselves as opposed to just randomly accepting every way in which we react. Your habits, your priorities, the ways in which you interact with the people and the work that you love, even how your perception is being shaped: all of this partially came from learning from your experiences. We are the sum of our experiences, hence they are priceless. What you and I are today is due to what we have experienced and how we decided to label that. If nurtured, this process of learning from your experience can either promulgate progress by repeating what you liked in the past, or simply never bring the good stuff back again.

2. Always dedicate some time just for thinking.

Dedicate some time for yourself where you can just escape the clutter and sit down and think. That's how we learn about what we want from life… about what it is that makes us enjoy it even more… what pushes us more and more towards success and improvement. And learning from your experiences means taking all of that and bringing it back into your life.

3. Learn from your experiences but try learning from others as well.

First you need to find a couple of people whom you admire for some reason, then you take a notebook and write down what it is that you like about them - their discipline, their passion, their dedication, how they talk to people, how they dress, their ideas about leisure and enjoying their spare time. Finally you take the notebook and pick which of those values you will embed in your own life - which of those experiences you will try to bring to your life, too. Prioritise, set, and go. See which standards, values and experiences lead towards improvement and success and try and make them a point of your life. Learn from your experiences over and over.

YOU CANNOT CREATE EXPERIENCE

Bad experiences suck: bad situations you can't control are going to be part of life. One way to enhance learning is by doing. If you want to learn how to drive a car then you go through experiencing some situations: you find out the more you drive the more you get better at it. Since mistakes are often quite jarring to someone who cares about what they are doing people naturally work hard to avoid them. No one likes to fail. It is basic to human nature to try to do better and this means attempting to explain one's failures well enough so that they can be remedied.

TIPS

1. Find a meaning.

Ask yourself how you can use the bad experience. Viktor E Frankl in his book *Man's Search for Meaning* found meaning in his suffering while in a Nazi concentration camp. Here are some ways you can find a meaning in a bad experience and to move past it:

- What has it taught you?
- Has it made you stronger/kinder/wiser?

- Even simply enduring a bad moment has meaning in making your happy moments better.

2. Keep a failure log.

Keep track of any failures, embarrassments or blunders. Using a failure log you can give you a little check mark of accomplishment. It may seem odd to reward failures in this way, but rewarding your failures serves two main purposes:

- It makes you more willing to take chances when the only risk is to your pride.
- It causes you to focus more on learning and growth than on external recognition.

3. Find a new goal.

Don't dwell in the past. The best way to get out of a rut is to start building momentum again. Get a new goal or pursuit. A new challenge will get you to stop thinking about your failure and get you to focus on something positive. A new goal will also give you the opportunity for future successes instead of dwelling on a current stumble.

4. Remove chronic sources of stress.

Your ability to handle big stresses depends on how well you handle the little ones. If your life is constantly driving you crazy you need to reconstruct it to better handle stress.

5. Build a support base.

Building a support base of colleagues and mentors will help you when times are rough. This is definitely a situation where you need to prepare in advance. Even if you do not have to deal with a particularly difficult situation right now, you might need some reinforcement in the future.

6. Be humble.

A sense of humility and humour can keep you moving forward when things are tough. Being humble in your abilities but confident in your chances to grow will let you shrug off failures, and being humble doesn't necessarily mean you have low self-esteem. It just means you are focused more on doing things without expecting immediate success. Many eastern philosophies emphasise goalless action. This doesn't mean that you should not strive for anything, but that you should detach yourself from the outcome. If you win, great: if you lose, then you are one step closer.

7. Stop analysing and start doing something new.

There is a maximum limit to how much you learn from an experience. That limit is actually fairly small within an isolated incident. If you give one speech -

and it fails - you might be able to learn one or two points of improvement. Anything you learn after this threshold is just speculation (which is often incorrect). After you have gathered a couple of learning points, stop: start doing something new. Pick out a new goal and move forward. After all, isn't that what failures are for? To give you a small learning point and direct you towards bigger and better things.

WE ARE ALL THE PRODUCT OF ALL OUR EXPERIENCES

We all are shaped by the experiences in our lives. And the memories, good and bad, have permanently altered our outlook towards our lives and futures. Our responses to situations and events in our lives are all shaped by our experiences. Our thought processes, mindsets, attitudes, aspirations, expectations and social behaviours are all altered or shaped by our experiences. Many of our experiences are usually personal in nature and there are several experiences that are conceived. The personal experiences that we hold on to for longer are usually deeper in nature because we have endured them personally - as opposed to the ones that are conceived by other people's personal experiences or opinions, which change over time and are not based on our individual personal experiences.

TIPS

1. Dreaming about the world. The world we experience around us is no more out there than our dreams.

2. We may find it hard to come to terms with the fact that our normal waking experiences of reality are a manifestation within the mind, but in many other instances we readily accept that we create our experiences.

3. The story of our lives is written by the remembering self.

We are all born with a unique genetic blueprint, which lays out the basic characteristics of our personality as well as our physical health and appearance... and yet, we all know that life experiences do change us.

(Joan D Vinge).

Third Chapter

Embrace Failure

Failures are finger posts on the road to achievement (C S Lewis).

Many of life's failures are people who did not realise how close they were to success when they gave up (Thomas Edison).

If you are not failing every now and again, it's a sign you're not doing anything very innovative (Woody Allen).

Do not be embarrassed by your failures, learn from them and start again (Richard Branson).

It's fine to celebrate success but it is more important to heed the lessons of failure (Bill Gates).

The word embrace means to eagerly accept or to be serious about starting something new. To embrace can mean different things to different people in different contents.

DO NOT BE EMBARRASSED BY YOUR FAILURES

Failures can happen to the best of us. In fact, sometimes these failures can turn into opportunities. If you fail at an endeavour you need to own it and hone it. Own the failure and admit you are that aware it was made. Then put measures in place to correct the failure. Some failures are one-time incidents, while others are long-range. Long-range failures usually result from the poor habits that were previously created.

Learning from failures requires two very important criteria. First, you need to be able to take responsibility for your actions: this may be easier said than done. Second, those who do not learn from history are doomed to repeat it. Listen to constructive criticism and come up with an alternative plan for the next time you are in the same situation.

TIPS

1. Accepting responsibility makes learning possible.
2. Don't equate making failures with hard work.
3. You can't change failures but you can choose how to respond to them.
4. Growth starts when you can see room for improvement.
5. Work to understand why it happened and what the factors were.

6. What information could have helped you avoid this failure?
7. What kinds of changes are required to avoid making this failure again?

QUITTING IS NOT AN OPTION

We all face difficult times at some point in our lives. Sometimes challenges comes in waves, with one hardship or misfortune following another. In reality, dealing with horrible events is clearly not simple or easy. Nonetheless, empowering yourself by accepting the situation, dealing with it as best you can and reminding yourself that happiness may still be possible will be the first step to feeling better.

Next, it can be easy and quite understandable to focus almost exclusively on bad or truly horrible experiences. It can be helpful to acknowledge the simple truth - that horrible things happen and are unfortunately part of life. Quitting is not an option.

<u>TIPS</u>

1. Courage.

It is the first of human qualities, because it is the quality which guarantees all other qualities.

2. Perceived control.

Tough timers view failure from a position of control. They understand life in terms of control. They understand life in terms of things they can control and things they cannot control. This paradoxical blend of seizing and yielding builds their confidence for dealing with tough times.

3. Problem ownership.

Tough timers feel responsible for taking action, regardless of the cause of the adversity or whose problem it is. They would rather fix the problem than fix the blame.

4. Perseverance.

Tough timers persist until they win. They know that nothing great was ever accomplished by a quitter. They know, at a gut level, that there is a time limit on tough times.

HOW TO GET OVER FAILURE AND MOVE ON

It is unfortunate that, in societies obsessed with success and achievement, failure can be made to feel like the worst thing that could ever happen to a person. The reality is that failure is commonplace but so is overcoming it and so is pushing through to move towards successful endeavours in the future. No one likes to fail, whether it's at work or home, but failure is a normal part of life. If you never ever suffer a failure, then you're probably not pushing yourself to your full potential.

TIPS

1. Remain calm.

Whatever you're feeling about a failure, don't lose your composure over it. Look at it this way - it won't make any difference to the outcome whether you blow your top or stay calm but it will take a lot less energy and will maintain your reputation if you choose the latter response.

2. Take your time.

People don't usually recover from a large failure overnight. It takes time for the emotions to heal.

3. Stop worrying. Start laughing.

Yes, the sun will come up again tomorrow. Yes, things might be miserable for a little while but how will worry help?

4. Review what your failure has taught you.

There are always things to take away from a failure, to inform your future direction. It might also be the case that you have created your future direction. It could potentially be that you have made the failure seem worse than it is: partial failure is also partial success and if you can draw out what was successful and build on that then the sense of having failed lessens. Sociologist Hugh Mackay believes that we don't value failure in the way we ought to.

5. Stay in the present.

Author Leo Babauta suggests that the response needed is to:

- Just do it, now, in the moment.
- Bring yourself back in the moment and focus on what you're doing right at this moment.

6. Remember other people fail, too.

Most people don't talk openly about their failures. Lots of people fail time and time again before meeting with success. Thomas Edison failed 10,000 times before he invented the electric light bulb.

7. You are not your mistakes.

Life didn't come with instructions. Accept that mistakes will happen. You are not your mistakes. You are not your struggles. You are here now, with the power to shape your day and your tomorrow.

8. Life's best lessons are learned at unexpected times.

We don't seek many of the greatest lessons we learn in life on purpose. Life's best lessons are usually learned at the worst times.

9. Life goes on.

Failures are painful when they happen, but years later this collection of failures - called experience - leads to success. If it's good, it's going to be wonderful. If it's bad, it's going to be an experience.

10. You can't see the whole parade from where you stand.

You never know from where you stand whether what you are experiencing will turn out to be good or bad until enough time has passed.

Failure should be our teacher, not our undertaker. Failure is delay, not defeat. It is a temporary detour, not a dead end. Failure is something we can avoid only by saying nothing, doing nothing, and being nothing.

(Denis Waitley).

Fourth Chapter

Second Chance

Having a second chance makes you want to work even harder (Tia Mowry).

We all have big changes in our lives that are more or less a second chance (Harrison Ford).

If you don't design your own life plan, chances are you'll fall into someone else's plan. And guess what they have planned for you? Not much (Jim Rohn).

You have to learn the rules of the game. And then you have to play better than anyone else (Albert Einstein).

The term second chance is usually used to describe an opportunity after a first similar opportunity has been squandered or lost through adverse circumstances. Similarly, the expression is used to describe a situation where a person has a second opportunity to achieve something: a pass mark in an exam paper; an educational qualification; a driving licence or establishing a business – something that they were not able to achieve at the first attempt.

WHEN HOPE IS LOST

You are not alone if you feel like giving up on your dreams, your hopes, and - for some - even on life. I want you to know that we all feel that way. You are in good company if you have failed at something. Every person who has done great things has failed on their way to success. If you've been put down, told you'll never make it, have felt like everyone else is doing better than you - you're not alone. It usually seems that right when you have the most hopeless moments of your life it is always right before something amazing is going to happen.

TIPS

1. You never fail until you're satisfied with failure.

Failure is not falling down; failure is staying down when you have the choice to get back up. Sometimes you have to fail a thousand times to succeed, which means you haven't really failed yet - you've just found a bunch of ways that don't work. So don't get so hung up on a few failed attempts that you miss every new opportunity coming your way. All your ideas that don't work are simply stepping stones on your way to the one idea that does. As Winston Churchill once said, 'Success is not final; failure is not fatal: it is the courage to continue that counts.'

2. What you have learned is what's important.

Life always offers you a second chance - it's called tomorrow. But this second chance doesn't mean anything if you haven't learned from the events of today. You have to acknowledge your troubles but gather strength from them and laugh at your mistakes but learn from them. Getting a second chance in life is about giving yourself the opportunity to grow beyond your past failures. It's about learning as you go and positively adjusting your attitude and efforts towards future possibilities.

3. Tough times are just part of life's natural balance.

Life lives, life dies. Life laughs, life cries. Life gives up and life tries and life looks different through everyone's eyes. In fact who you were, who you are and who you will become are three completely different people.

4. Pain helps you grow.

Sometimes things must change so you can change. Sometimes you must break a little so you can get a peek inside to see what an awesome powerhouse you are. Sometimes mistakes must be made so wisdom can be earned.

5. Success is a way of living.

Don't let your struggles become your identity. Not everything in your life will go as you expect it to. This is why you need to drop expectations, live in the present and go with the flow rather than against it. Remind yourself that it's perfectly okay not to be perfect. Ultimately, success is not something you achieve, it is what you learn and how you grow as you deal with the realities of life - it is a way of living and being.

6. You can choose differently.

The difference between a mountain and a molehill is your perspective. And, in many cases, the only thing in life you have control over is your perspective. No matter what happens you control what the meaning is - and what to do with the meaning you give to the circumstance.

7. It's not supposed to be easy.

Just because you're not where you want to be today doesn't mean you won't be there some day. Again, success is tied to long-term determination. Successful people keep moving and trying. They make mistakes but they do not quit.

8. Life is still good.

You may have seen better days - but you have also seen worse. You might not have all your wants - but you do have all your needs. You woke up with a few pains - but you woke up. Your life may not be perfect - but it is good. And more good things are coming down the road - as long as you keep moving forward.

HOW TO REMAIN HOPEFUL

When life is going smoothly and we're getting our needs met, it's easy to feel hopeful and be optimistic. The key is to find a sustained hope when life is presenting us with challenges, difficulties and obstacles. Where within yourself do you find and access hope when life is dishing out lemons? Well, here's something you should know: somewhere within each of us lies the belief that whatever it is you wish for or want can become a reality.

<u>TIPS</u>

1. Build positive beliefs in your abilities.

Research has demonstrated that good self-esteem plays an important role in coping with stress and recovering from difficult events. It reminds you of your strengths and accomplishments.

2. Find a sense of purpose in your life.

In the face of crisis or tragedy, finding a sense of purpose can play an important role in recovery.

3. Be optimistic.

Staying optimistic during dark periods can be difficult, but maintaining a hopeful outlook is an important part. What you are dealing with may be difficult, but it is important to remain hopeful and positive about a brighter future.

4. Nurture yourself.

When you're stressed it can be all too easy to neglect your own needs. Losing your appetite and not getting enough sleep are both common reactions to a crisis situation. Focus on building yourself nurturance skills, even when you are troubled.

5. Develop your problem-solving skills.

Research suggests that people who are able to come up with solutions to a problem are better able to cope with problems than those who are not. Whenever you encounter a new challenge make a quick list of some of the potential ways you could solve the problem.

6. Take steps to solve problems.

Simply waiting for a problem to go away on its own only prolongs the crisis. Instead, start working on resolving the issue immediately. While there may not be any fast or simple solutions you can take steps towards making your situation better and less stressful.

HOW TO ACHIEVE BETTER THAN THE FIRST TIME

We all need second chances. This isn't a perfect world. We're not perfect people. I'm probably on my billionth second chance right now and I'm not ashamed to admit it. Because even though I've failed a lot it means I've tried a lot, too.

We rarely get things right the first time. Almost every major accomplishment in a person's life starts with the decision to try again - to get up after every failed attempt and give it another shot. The only difference between an opportunity and an obstacle is attitude. Getting a second chance in life is about giving yourself the opportunity to grow beyond your past failures. Challenge yourself to be who you know you are capable of being. Challenge yourself to follow through - to walk your talk.

TIPS

1. Let go of the past.

Every difficult moment in our lives is accompanied by an opportunity for personal growth and creativity. But - in order to attain this growth and creativity - we must first learn to let go of the past. We must recognise that difficulties pass like everything else in life. And, once they pass, all we're left with are our unique experiences and the lessons required to make a better attempt next time.

2. Identify the lesson.

Everything is a life lesson. Everyone you meet, everything you encounter - they're all part of the learning experience we call life. Never forget to acknowledge the lesson, especially when things don't go your way.

3. Lose the negative attitude.

Negative thinking creates negative results. Positive thinking creates positive results. The mind must believe it can do something before it is capable of actually doing it.

4. Figure out what you really want.

Don't quit just because you didn't get it right on your first shot. And don't waste your life fulfilling someone else's dreams and desires. You must follow your intuition and make a decision to never give up on who you are capable of becoming.

5. Maintain self-control and work on it for real.

If you want a real second chance you've got to be willing to give it all you've got.

My whole story is just about me having a second chance. (Two Chainz)

Fifth Chapter

Struggle

If there is no struggle, there is no progress (Frederick Douglass).

Once all struggle is grasped, miracles are possible (Mao Zedong).

The battle of life is, in most cases, fought uphill; and to win it without a struggle were perhaps to win it without honour. If there were no difficulties there would be no success; if there were nothing to struggle for, there would be nothing to be achieved (Samuel Smiles).

To struggle can be defined as: to make strenuous efforts to achieve a desired outcome in the face of adversity or relentless opposition. To struggle is to proceed with great effort, perseverance, tenacity, consistency and an unperturbed focus on the achievement of the desired outcome. This means embracing the challenge presenting itself and taking the initiative and the opportunity to achieve the desired outcome.

HOW TO STAY STANDING IN TIMES OF STRUGGLE

Unfortunately a struggle is something which every single one of us has to go through at some point in our lives. It can hold us back, it can damage our motivation and it can basically feel like we are stuck - with no way out. You just have to understand the situation and look at it from a different perspective. Think of it as an outside situation: detach yourself from the situation in order to find a way out. If you've made a bad decision and are unhappy with your circumstances, resolve to change direction. Effecting a correction can be difficult, but persisting in an unhappy state is torture. Everyone encounters struggles. No one is ever singled out. No one knows why some things happen; they just do. Some decide to regain their footing, catch their breath and keep walking forward. Others choose to give up.

Sometimes struggles comes to your life to suggest that it's time to change course. For example when someone leaves you there is no use blaming yourself. Instead you should take it as a sign that a newer and more enlightened relationship (which is more meaningful or constructive) should be sought.

Struggles are clever devices through which nature compels humanity - which includes you - to develop, expand and progress. It's either an ordeal or a magnificent experience, depending on your attitude towards it.

<u>TIPS</u>

1. Be aware - and accept - that struggle is inevitable in life. To avoid or resist it will only make it persist. Everywhere you look in the world there is unmistakable struggle.

2. Take inspiration and learn from others who have dealt successfully with struggle.

Examples:

Helen Keller: lost her sight and hearing due to a mysterious fever when she was only 18 months old. She overcame her deafness and blindness to become a strong, educated woman who spoke about and promoted women's rights.

Winston Churchill: overcame a stuttering problem and poor performance in school to become prime minister of the United Kingdom and one of the most influential political leaders of the 20th century. He was also known for his powerful and rousing speeches.

Wilma Rudolph: born prematurely, the 20th of 22 children. She overcame double pneumonia, scarlet fever and polio to become the winner of three track gold medals at the 1960 Rome Olympic Games.

THE BATTLE OF LIFE IS THROUGH STRUGGLE

No one can deny the fact that life in the world is one continuous struggle. The person who does not know the struggle of life is either an immature soul or a soul who has risen above the life of this world. The object of a human being in this world is to attain the perfection of humanity, and therefore it is necessary that man should go through what we call the struggle of life.

There are two different attitudes that people adopt while going through this struggle of life. One struggles along bravely through life; the other becomes disappointed, heartbroken, before arriving at his/her destination. As soon as a person loses the courage to go through the struggle of life the burden of the whole world falls upon his/her head. But the person who goes on struggling through life makes their way. The one whose patience is exhausted - the one who has fallen in this struggle - is trodden upon by those who walk through life. Even bravery and courage are not sufficient to go through the struggle of life: there is something else which must be studied and understood.

One must study the nature of life; one must understand the psychology of this struggle. In order to understand this struggle one must see that there are three sides to it: struggle with oneself, struggle with others and struggle with circumstances. One person may be capable of struggling with himself, but that is not sufficient. Another is able to struggle with others, but even that is not sufficient. A third person may answer the demands of circumstances, but this is not enough either. What is needed is that all three should be studied and learned - and one must be able to manage the struggle in all three directions.

And now the question is: where should one begin and where should one end? Generally one starts by struggling with others and then one struggles all through life - and never finishes. The one who is somewhat wiser struggles with conditions, and perhaps he accomplishes things a little better. But the one who struggles with himself first is the wisest, for once he has struggled with himself. Which is the most difficult struggle: the other struggles will become easy for him.

TIPS

1. Change.

To effectively move away from an unfavourable situation you must decide exactly where you wish to go. Create a formidable intention for yourself, and feed that intention with the passion and energy that's in your desire for change.

2. Problems.

There's no shortage of problems waiting to be addressed. When you see problems piled on top of problems - and when there seems to be no end to the work that must be done in order to resolve them - what are you really seeing? You're looking. You're looking at a situation in which you can truly make a difference. You're looking at an environment where you can reach great heights by raising the stakes and pulling the reality of what's possible along with you.

3. Achievement.

There is no shortcut to a great achievement. There is no substitute for doing the work. Meditate on this every day: I will do the work. As Einstein once said, 'Genius is 1 per cent talent and 99 per cent hard work.' You must run to be a runner. You must write to be a writer.

4. Focus.

Lack of focus is the most common problem that holds people back from their potential. We all have strengths and difficulties, and we all have the same 24-hour days and seven-day weeks to work with. If you find it difficult to deal with where you are, or how life is treating you, it's time to change focus.

5. Positive thinking.

The reality you live through daily is a process of your thinking. You are essentially who you design yourself to be -most of what you experience is the direct result of your own creation. This reality cannot be changed without first changing your thinking.

There are lots of inherent events in life that occur completely independently of you, but they do not have to cause ongoing confusion and suffering. They happen, you experience a little stress, you adjust and you move forward. When your mind clings to these events in a negative light and intensifies their significance into perpetuity you stay stuck and do not move forward at all.

6. Mistakes.

No matter what you're going to make mistakes: it's an unavoidable truth. But the good news is that if you follow your heart and intuition the mistakes you make will be steps in the right direction. Just because you fail once at something doesn't mean you're going to fail at everything. Keep trying, hold on and believe in yourself. Keep your head held high and your chin up.

7. Acceptance.

What you must realise is that you don't really need more time: you just need to appreciate life in the current time. It's a beautiful and bitter way of thinking all at once. If you don't have what you want now you don't have what you want, but you still have a lot. Be thankful for what is and also be thankful for what has not yet come to you, for that means there are still many possibilities available to you.

8. Present moment.

Regardless of what's happened in the past or what might happen in the future, it's being here now that's important. We can gain experience from the past, but we can't edit it. We can hope for the future, but we don't know if it will ever come. This moment - right now - is your life. Say 'Yes' to it. Don't ignore it by pretending that you're living in some other time and place.

HOW TO STAY MOTIVATED IN THE MIDST OF STRUGGLE

We all fall but we can get up. During this time of pain it is important to keep a momentum to keep going.

TIPS

1. Get excited.

Most people don't think about this much: get excited if you want to break out of a slump.

2. Build anticipation.

This will sound hard, and many people will skip this tip. But it really works.

3. Think about it daily.

If you think about your goal every day it is much more likely to become true.

4. Realise that there's an ebb and flow.

Motivation is not a constant thing which is always there for you. It comes and goes - and comes and goes again, like the tide. But realise that while it may go away, it doesn't do so permanently. It will come back.

5. Stick with it.

Whatever you do don't give up. Even if you aren't feeling any motivation today, or this week, don't give up. Ride out the ebbs and surf on the flows and you'll get there.

6. Call for help.

Call your mum or your best friend - it doesn't matter who - just tell them your problems, and talking about it will help.

7. Think about the benefits, not the difficulties.

One common problem is that we think about how hard something is: just thinking about it makes you tired. But instead of thinking about how hard something is think about what you will get out of it.

When you don't come from struggle, gaining appreciation is a quality that's difficult to come by. (Shania Twain).

Sixth Chapter

Opportunity

The world is all gates, all opportunities, strings of tension waiting to be struck (Ralph Waldo Emerson).

Opportunities are usually disguised as hard work, so most people don't recognise them (Ann Landers).

If you wait for opportunities to occur, you will be one of the crowd (Edward de Bono).

Opportunities are often things you haven't noticed the first time around (Catherine Deneuve).

Sometimes opportunities float right past your nose. Work hard, apply yourself, and be ready. When an opportunity comes you can grab it (Julie Andrews).

An opportunity can be defined as a favourable or advantageous circumstance or combination of circumstances to do or achieve a desired goal. At the social level people talk of a favourable or suitable occasion or time as an opportunity to carry out certain desired behaviour. In an occupational, professional or academic sense, an opportunity is often thought of as a chance for progress or advancement.

In Douglas Miller's book he states that the great thing is that our opportunities can come from almost anywhere. We often assume that opportunities come to us from the world around us. More often than not, however, they are conceived and born within our rich and varied imaginations - though we do need to connect with our inner world to find them.

These five words - **the possibility of doing something** - neatly define the psychology behind opportunities. Opportunities are only ever possibilities - they are never absolute. The difficulty here for many people is that they wait for the opportunity to become a certainty. We like to have all the information available to us which proves that the opportunity is the absolute certainty we want. We gain our security from what we believe to be the truth. But no opportunity is absolute. Perfect information does not exist. We risk the danger of opportunity paralysis because we want to know that the coast is clear before we venture out. The more we have to lose the more ready we are to go for it if the chink of light is shown to us. The challenge for us as opportunity spotters in affluent societies is to risk a part of what we have for the possibility, rather than for the certainty.

HOW TO UNLOCK OPPORTUNITIES

To be successful at anything you need to be able to recognise an opportunity when you see one. You need to be able to identify a problem or gap, and come up with a solution.

TIPS

1. Acknowledge the need for new opportunities.

You need to step up and decide that - whether in your career or your social life - things aren't all that they could be and that you need to find something new.

2. Take inspiration from others.

Recognise opportunities into lives of other people. Do some research into the circumstances that other people put themselves into. Discover opportunities. Behind every successful person is a story of hard work.

3. Strip yourself of bias.

If an opportunity presents itself that is outside of your norm our instinct is often to seek out the reasons not to pursue it. eg: it's too expensive, it's too dangerous.

4. Be willing to learn.

The greatest man or woman is he/she who learns because through learning we have new ideas, new patterns of thought revealed to us. When new ideas are revealed to us we can find ways in which we can improve ourselves.

5. Change your circle of friends.

Our circle of friends always influences what we become. Likewise, they also affect what we are exposed to. What would you like to become? Find people who are in your niche area and those people will tell you when new opportunities arise.

6. Be at the right place at the right time.

When we are at the right place at the right moment, opportunities fly to us effortlessly. Most of the people who have made it have not only made it because of their talents and abilities but also because they were at the right place and the right moment. Try to go to seminars, workshops or events that are related to your industry.

THE OPPORTUNITY MINDSET

- Curiosity: Opportunity desires a curious mind that is always asking deeper and more insightful questions.

- Generosity: Opportunity desires a generous heart that is willing to give opportunities to others.
- Perseverance: Opportunity desires someone who has determination, who will keep persisting and persevering despite the seemingly insurmountable obstacles that stand in their way.
- Confidence: Opportunity desires a confident demeanour - someone who never doubts their skills, strength, resources and abilities.
- Optimism: Opportunity desires an optimistic attitude that doesn't waver off course if things don't go as expected.
- Playfulness: Opportunity desires a lighthearted approach that is willing to be a little creative, willing to the outside the box and willing to break conventional rules.
- Responsibility: Opportunity desires someone who is fully committed and responsible for their decisions, behaviour and actions: someone who doesn't make excuses or throw blame on others.
- Hindsight: Opportunity desires someone with hindsight who can see beyond this fleeting moment into the future. This someone understands that what might look like a problem now might actually be a once-in-a-lifetime opportunity.

- Gratitude: Opportunity desires a grateful spirit which is thankful for anything that life throws its way, no matter how dark or grim it might seem on the surface.

HOW TO LEARN FROM FAILED OPPORTUNITIES

Sometimes you can become so distraught due to the fact that things have gone wrong. One of the best things is to reflect on all those times when things didn't go as planned and to distil the lessons you should have learned. This allows us to make certain that we are learning as many lessons as we can from all our experiences and setting ourselves up for success in the future.

TIPS

1. There is no such thing as failure.

Yes, things can go wrong or not according to plan, but really there is no such thing as failure because there is always a very good reason why things didn't work out and a lesson you need to learn.

2. If you want something for the wrong reasons it will never work out the way you want it to in the end.

3. You can use the fact that things didn't initially go as you desired as one of your greatest motivators for success in the future.

4. In one way or another persistence, dedication and hard work always eventually pay off.

5. After something goes wrong, if you choose to look for the lessons and turn your attention to improving at whatever it is you were trying to do instead of getting frustrated you really can dramatically and immediately improve your performance and take things to the next level.

6. After you fail three of the best things you should do are:

    - Explore the reasons why.
    - Be open to learning.
    - If it is something you really want - and just feel you were meant to do - then immediately recommit to trying again.

7. It's better to try, take chances and not succeed than it is to just sit back and wonder what would have happened because you are afraid to fail.

8. The only bad thing that can result from failing is if you lose the courage to try again.

9. There's no need to be embarrassed, because every single person fails at something at some point in their life. You are not alone.

10. Some of the best growth happens as a result of things going wrong. Go for what you want. You have nothing to lose and so many things to gain.

HOW OPPORTUNITIES ARE CREATED

Opportunity is all around us but yet at the same time sometimes we never see it. In Baron's article he says that an opportunity involves the potential to create something new: here the word created refers to the method in which the opportunity was realised.

TIPS

1. Keep the right mindset: you can create opportunities if you take charge of your career.
2. Have self-knowledge: know your values, skills, strengths, weaknesses and passions.
3. Hone your knowledge and skills: perfect them in your area of expertise.
4. Possess the ability to analyse opportunities: make sound decisions.

5. Maintain resilience: success is rarely immediate.
6. Stay flexible: when you take the initiative good things happen, but sometimes they aren't what you intended. Be flexible towards what life throws your way.

High achievers spot rich opportunities swiftly, make big decisions quickly and move into action immediately. Follow these principles and you can make your dreams come true.

(Robert H Schuller).

Seventh Chapter

The Successful Person

You have reached the pinnacle of success as soon as you become uninterested in money, compliments, or publicity (Thomas Wolfe).

Some people dream of success while others wake up and work hard at it (Winston Churchill).

Successful people have a target and goals: they understand there is one fundamental in life. You need to understand where you are aiming so that you can start shooting towards it. It's having a target and the shot is your actions towards that target (Preston Waters).

Success means a lot of things to many individuals. This all depends on a multitude of factors, including these questions: who is making the judgement? And against what yardstick is the judgement being made? In addition, it is also important to ascertain whether or not the judge and the judged are in mutual agreement about the method of judgement. Nevertheless, it is fair to say that in general everyday social life, a person is described as successful on the basis of their personal achievements in one or more aspects of life. Having cash, owning property or excelling at an endeavour will mean success, and this is a word pregnant with too much meaning.

I will define success as being able to do something so well that you are filled with joy at its accomplishment. It's the inner drive which comes from wanting to do so well: being able to weave your way through a maze of those determined to defend the opposition/the opposing point of view and delivering the goods. Success is triumph in the midst of opposition. How successful one is can be determined by the size of the opposition: being able to withstand that opposition just adds to how much you could have mastered success.

So often we hear of success being attributed to people - say footballers or singers - not because of their riches but because of how adept they have become in their speciality. Some will say how much success these people have found, not in their riches but in their domain. Equating success to how many material things people possess is flirting because one success today will not be the success of tomorrow - this is relative success.

How can one measure success? It can be measured by how many elements are accomplished in doing a task. It's the inner fulfilment one gets at doing the right things at the right time. One gets partial success when accomplishing tasks partially and full success when accomplishing tasks fully. No one needs money to be successful but successful people attract money to themselves.

ATTRIBUTES OF A SUCCESSFUL PERSON

Warren Buffet has been successful at investing and building long-term businesses. Bill Gates has been successful at creating a software empire that has changed the way we use computers. If you want to achieve your life's dream and be wildly successful you need to model yourself after people who are living their dream. The more qualities you have in common the higher your chances for being wildly successful.

We all start out in life as being quite ordinary and many remain that way. The few who have become extraordinary have these attributes (or these are things that you could observe about them):

1. Defined aim, vision and purpose.

Successful people constantly seek clarity in their lives. They know what they want and they follow their own dream. Vague desires and beliefs lead to vague outcomes. It is this sense of direction that gives them the staying power to stick to their goals and achieve their dreams.

2. Expertise and excellence.

No matter what they pursue they become the best in their field. There is no job too small for them and successful people strive for excellence. They pursue mastery and understand that money is a product of the value they offer.

3. Focus.

People who experience success know how to concentrate. They realise that they cannot do everything and they focus on the activities that will give them the highest return on the goals they want to achieve.

4. Positive attitude and perseverance.

Extraordinary people have realistic optimism: realistic because they take action and optimistic because no matter what the result may be they believe their success is inevitable.

5. Flexibility.

One misconception that ordinary people have about persevering is staying the course no matter what. This is true only if the reason for pursuing your goal is still valid. Most successful people became successful doing something different from what they initially intended to do, eg, Steve Jobs started with computers then went into animation and really made his comeback with the iPod. This is normal because the world is always changing and these people know a lot more now than when they started.

6. Mastery of time.

Successful people are successful because they get a lot done. The only way to do that is by making the most out of the allotted 24 hours we all get. Extraordinary people value their time and see the direct connection between how they spend their time and their well-being.

7. Strong communication skills.

They are experts at building rapport and separate what is being said from the meaning they put into what is being said.

8. Courage.

Successful people have the courage to begin and the courage to continue. They are not afraid to burn bridges if it means moving forward.

9. Giving.

Successful people are generous givers. They know and believe in the secret that the more you give the more you receive - as long as you are genuine about your gifts. They operate on the principle expressed by Zig Ziglar's quote that you will get all you want in life if you just help enough other people get what they want.

10. High self-esteem.

Extraordinary people believe that they deserve their success and know that they can do anything they set their mind to. They understand that a mistake is something that they have made and not who they are.

11. Action-oriented.

Successful people are doers, not talkers. They don't wait for conditions to be perfect before they take action. They just go for it, observe the feedback and then modify their next action accordingly.

12. Confidence.

Successful people take action, and they understand that the first time you do something is always the hardest and all subsequent times will get easier. Success is the combination of confidence with competence.

13. Reading.

Most - if not all- successful people like to read. If you believe that success leaves clues and that you can be successful by thinking and acting like a successful person, then reading should be a part of your daily life. It is important to read the books that will make the most difference to you.

14. Having big dreams.

Sir Richard Branson, Walt Disney and Sam Walton all had big dreams and for the most part achieved more than they originally imagined. This is one of the reasons they became successful. They were not afraid to dream big and then go for it.

15. Well-rounded and balanced.

Truly successful people strive to be successful in all aspects of their lives. They live healthy lives, become financially independent, nurture meaningful relationships, develop personal mastery and accomplish their professional goals.

16. Enthusiasm.

A sure sign of someone extraordinary is the enthusiasm they have about their passion and their life. They wake up in the morning excited about their day because they know it is going to bring them one step closer to achieving their dream.

17. The mindset of abundance.

Successful people don't view happiness or success as a finite resource, where achieving happiness and success for yourself means denying someone else happiness and success. They believe that there is enough to go around and it is more about creating value and not competition.

18. Good character.

Heroes are people who triumph. They all act in honesty and integrity.

19. Great company.

Test this by looking at people you know and the people they hang out with. Surround yourself with people living the life you want to live and adopt their beliefs and habits.

20. Energy-consciousness.

Those who become great understand that successfully managing their energy is just as important - if not more so - than managing their time. One of the most important principles in energy management is knowing that rest is as important as action. Successful people are aware that low energy produces poor results and this violates their need for excellence.

ACQUIRE SUCCESS

Many people want to achieve success in life, but it's easier said than done. There are so many distractions that it can be challenging to discipline oneself to accomplish a monumental goal. There are no short cuts when it comes to being successful - just a series of strategies that, if applied, will ensure you get ahead of the game. You just need to learn how to acquire: as long as you keep moving, someday you'll reach where you're going. Never give up.

TIPS

1. You, the strengths and qualities you possess at the moment.

If you are qualified or have a skill, that's the best place to start. Use those skills and - if you are not qualified - all is not lost. Acquire that qualification - it's never too late.

2. Change.

Even if you are starting with a disadvantage you can make it up.

3. Positivity.

All successful people believe in themselves and in the rightness of what they are doing. Positivity is infectious and rubs off on people around you.

BUILD SUCCESS

Opportunity in life never just shows up at your door and asks to come in. The only way you can achieve great success in life is by freeing your mind of all negative thoughts and putting down on paper exactly what you want to achieve in the next five years of your life. Why use five years as a good time frame? Because that is usually how many years it actually takes to turn a realistic but lofty dream into reality.

TIPS

1. Imagine becoming successful.

Einstein said imagination is more important than knowledge. The more vividly and accurately you imagine your success the easier it will be for the rest of yourself to follow through.

- Dedicate a few minutes every day to imagining your success. Imagine yourself in a movie in which you are successful.
- Cultivate a wealthy motivation when imagining your success. Successful people all believe in themselves and their missions.

2. Find the purpose.

Identify the things you love to do - the things that give you satisfaction. Once you identify what you love to do… use this information to find the purpose of your life or the objective of your life.

3. Define the meaning of success as you see it.

You cannot have success if you do not know what it means for you. Everyone views success differently and using someone else's standard for success is like eating another person's lunch or dinner and expecting to love it.

4. Identify the skills/materials needed to achieve your success.

If you want to be a famous speaker, for example, you need a broad vocabulary, subject knowledge, speech writing and presentation skills – and a clear voice.

5. Find a mentor.

A mentor is someone - usually with a bit more experience than you - who knows how to offer advice and who helps you in your pursuit. There are mentors behind many successful people.

A mentor will help you:

- Network - making connections with people who have connections. Contrary to popular belief, networking is mutually beneficial. You offer expertise, your opinion or an opportunity to someone in exchange for something back.

- Troubleshoot - your mentor can help you figure out what you need to change in order to make your idea even better.
- Strategise - a mentor will probably have more vision than you because he/she's been in the game longer, with more successes and failures. You can draw on his or her legacy of experience to strategise about the future.

Would you like me to give you a formula for success? It's simple, really. Double your rate of failure. You are thinking of failure as the enemy of success. But it is not at all. You can be discouraged by failure or you can learn from it, so go ahead and make mistakes, make all you can. Because remember that is where you will find success

(Thomas J Watson).

Eighth Chapter

The Unsuccessful Person

No one can make you feel inferior without your consent (Eleanor Roosevelt).

If you don't value your time, neither will others. Stop giving away your time and talents. Value what you know and start charging for it (Kim Garst).

I have not failed. I've just found 10,000 ways that won't work (Thomas Edison).

To talk of an unsuccessful person gives the impression that the person has completely squandered their opportunities to achieve their desired goals in the aspect of being judged and that they will never be able to achieve the task or standard required. This would be appropriate when describing the efforts of deceased people or people who may not have had further opportunities - or a second chance - as a result of their age, health or some other factors.

UNSUCCESSFUL PERSON ATTRIBUTES

1. False beliefs.

These are incorrect ideas you hold about something or about yourself. An example of a false belief could be: 'I could never find a job in such a company.' False beliefs act as limiters to your true potential and so to your success. Getting rid of false beliefs and knowing more about them is the most important task that you should do if you are serious about success.

2. External locus of control.

This is the way of thinking that makes a person assume that everything which happens to him/her is the result of external factors. For example, thinking that the high unemployment rate is the reason you can't find a job is an example of the external locus of control. The flip side to that way of thinking is the internal locus of control, which is the way of thinking that makes you believe that you are in charge and in control of everything that happens to you. No successful person has an external locus of control, so - if you are serious about success - you should learn how to change your way of thinking from it being based on an external locus of control to it being based on an internal locus of control.

3. Lack of persistence.

What is good about having many qualities and skills if you lose the hope of succeeding after failing once or twice? The only people who succeed in life are the persistent ones: those who continue working right to the end until they get what they want, even if everything was against them and even if they failed many times.

4. Lack of flexibility.

Flexibility is the ability to adapt to external conditions. It's the ability to try something else or another method when your current method fails. The more flexible you are the more you will adapt to changes and the higher your chances of success will be.

5. Lack of planning.

If you don't have goals or plans then you are going to be a part of other people's plans.

6. Lack of self-confidence.

If you don't have strong self-confidence then - most probably - you will be too shy of presenting your ideas and you may give up your dreams as soon as someone tells you that they are not possible. You may fear taking any risks and so ignore many opportunities that could have made you successful.

7. Thinking that you lack resources.

Don't fool yourself by thinking that you lack resources because if you are serious about success you will do it without having any resources.

8. Success-related fears.

The types of fear that can affect your ability to succeed are the fear of failure and the fear of success. While they both seem to be complete opposites they can still have the same effect on you, which is preventing you from trying and so leading you to failure.

FEARING CHANGE

Fear can be an immobilising emotion and, if not managed correctly, can rob you of many opportunities and prevent you from creating and enjoying an abundant life. Here is an acronym for fear:

F = False

E = Evidence

A = Appearing

R = Real

We create false evidence in our minds to justify our decision not to move forward. We also become so overwhelmed with fear that we lose focus and lose sight of what is really important to us. This single factor can keep us in our current situation and we just carry on living our lives in their current state.

Fear is one of the strongest, most primitive emotions: scientists believe that there is even a kind of early warning system in the amygdala (the part of the brain that governs emotion) which allows us to experience fear before we have consciously become aware of the thing we are afraid of. A key difference between successful and unsuccessful people is that successful people initiate and control more of the changes in their lives. They decide where they want to be today, this week, this month, next year, 10 years from now, 30 years from now… and they take actions designed to achieve that result. Unsuccessful people tend to be more passive: they take what life - or other people - throws at them and, as a result, often lead constricted, embittered lives that don't reflect their authentic values and needs.

Steven Pressfield writes like this: 'I was crushed. Here I was, 42 years old, divorced, childless, having given up all normal human pursuits to chase the dream of being a writer. I'm a loser, my life is worthless.' However, he was quickly set right by a wise friend who said, 'Be happy. You're where you wanted to be, aren't you? So you're taking few blows. That's the price for being in the arena and not on the sidelines. Stop complaining and be grateful.'

At some point we all have to learn to take responsibility for our failure and look objectively at our personal limitations. The law of feedback states:

there is no failure; there is only feedback. Successful people look at mistakes as outcomes or results, not as failure. Unsuccessful people look at mistakes as permanent and personal.

Buckminster Fuller wrote: 'Whatever humans have learned had to be learned as a consequence only of trial and error experience. Humans have learned only through mistakes. Most people self-limit themselves. Most people do not achieve a fraction of what they are capable of achieving because they are afraid to try because they are afraid they will fail.'

TIPS

1. Take action.

Take bold, decisive action. Do something scary. Fear of failure immobilises you. To overcome this fear, you must act. When you act, act boldly. Action gives you the power to change the circumstances or the situation. You must overcome the inertia by doing something.

Dr Robert Schuller asks: 'What would you do if you knew you could not fail? What could you achieve? Be brave and just do it. If it doesn't work out the way you want, then do something else. But do something now.'

2. Persist.

Successful people just don't give up. They keep trying different approaches to achieving their outcomes until they finally get the results they want.

Unsuccessful people try one thing that doesn't work and then give up. Often people give up when they are on the threshold of succeeding.

3. Don't take failure personally.

Failure is about behaviour, outcomes, and results. Failure is not a personality characteristic. Although what you do may not give you the result you wanted it doesn't mean you are a failure. Because you made a mistake doesn't mean that you are a failure.

4. Do things differently.

If what you are doing isn't working do something else. There is an old saying: if you always do what you've always done, you'll always get what you always got. If you're not getting the results you want then you must do something different. Most people stop doing anything at all, and this guarantees they won't be successful.

5. Don't be so hard on yourself.

Hey, if nothing else, you know what doesn't work. Failure is a judgement or evaluation of behaviour. Look at failure as an event or a happening, not as a person.

6. Treat the experience as an opportunity to learn.

Think of failure as a learning experience. What did you learn from the experiences that will help you in the future? How can you use the experience to improve yourself or your situation? Ask yourself these questions:

- What was the mistake?
- Why did it happen?
- How could it have been prevented?
- How can I do better next time?

Then use what you learned from the experience to do things differently so that you get different results next time. Learn from the experience or ignore it.

7. Look for possible opportunities that result from the experience. Napoleon Hill, author of *Think and Grow Rich,* says that every adversity, every failure and every heartache carries with it the seed of an equivalent or a greater benefit. Look for the opportunity and the benefit.

8. Fail forward fast.

Tom Peters, the management guru, says that in today's business world companies must fail forward fast. What he means is that the way we learn is by making mistakes, so if we want to learn at a faster pace we must make mistakes at a faster pace. The key is that you must learn from the mistakes you make so you don't repeat them.

LACK OF UNDERSTANDING OF THE CONCEPT OF HARD WORK

While studying the biographies of Thomas Edison, Walt Disney and Ralph Lauren I found out that they understood hard work: they had fire burning from within even when there was yet nothing to show for it. They knew that success doesn't come to you: you work towards it. And in your journey towards success you'll have to be able to make it through the night - not the 12-hour sort of night – but, instead, nights that may linger for months or even years… nights when you'll have to keep working hard without seeing any visible result… nights when you'll have to deal with the negative attitudes of some people around who doesn't understand what you stand for… nights when it seems as if your dreams are almost impossible but you still keep working towards it…

Successful people know that during the period when achieving a goal starts getting difficult and maybe hopeless at times, that's when they ought to be working even more - that's the period called night and it is gloomy and the exact opposite of a rosy situation. You don't become successful simply by deciding to be successful. You work for it… work for it to the point where your goal just has no more option other than to give in to your demand. At some point we will all have to deal with our vulnerabilities, uncertainties and failures. Some of us trust that if we can keep moving forward, despite those challenges, we will be able to figure it all out with time.

While working hard is a virtue, it also has some basic failings. The hard work principle lends itself to measuring how hard or long you work instead of what you are getting done.

TIPS

1. Understand that successful people start from scratch.

2. Let go of unreasonable fears. Think 'I'm doing something that most people are not willing to do - that's why I'm ahead of them.'

3. Understand that only by taking action will you be able to move things forward.

4. Start out small. For example, if you want to become a public speaker, you don't have to start by speaking to an audience of thousands of people. Start in front of your friends and family members, and then expand from there.

5. If you have a blog, start interviewing people. Start a podcast and - at some point - have your own webinars on the topic you are good at.

6. Take consistent action, preferably on a daily basis.

The future is not a result of choices among alternative paths offered by the present, but a place that is created - created first in the mind and will, created next in activity. The future is not some place we are going to, but one we are creating. The paths are not to be found, but made, and the activity of making them changes both the maker and the destination (John Schaar).

Ninth Chapter

Turning Point

The river is constantly turning and bending and you never know where it's going to go and where you'll wind up. Following the bend in the river and staying on your own path means that you are on the right track. Don't let anyone deter you from that (Eartha Kitt).

The greatest revolution in our generation is that of human beings who, by changing the inner attitudes of their minds, can change the outer aspects of their lives (Marilyn Ferguson).

Really, it comes down to your philosophy. Do you want to play it safe and be good or do you want to take a chance and be great (Jimmy J)

Let him who would enjoy a good future waste none of his present (Roger Babson).

ONLY YOU CAN CHANGE YOUR LIFE

Taking ownership is the starting block from which great change can be achieved. You are the only person who can change your life: you are not beholden to anyone else for that change.

We experience many turning points in our lives, whenever we shift direction this way or that - maybe about an education or career choice. Some turning points are conscious, others less so. Some may be imposed by family or by other persuasive people. But all involve turning away from one path and towards another, and they shape and define the self that experience has made you.

TIPS

1. Practise empathy.

Make it a habit to try to place yourself in the shoes of another person.

2. Practise compassion.

Once you can understand another person and feel what they're going through, learn to want to end their suffering… and when you can, take even a small action to somehow ease their suffering in some way.

3. How would you want to be treated?

You should treat someone else exactly as you want them to treat you.

4. Be friendly.

When in doubt, follow this tip.

5. Be helpful.

Don't be blind to the needs and troubles of others. Look to help even before you're asked.

6. Overcome prejudice.

We all have our prejudices but try to see each person as an individual human being, with different backgrounds and needs and dreams.

THE FUTURE IS NOT SOME PLACE WE ARE GOING TO, BUT ONE WE ARE CREATING

From our own individual perspectives there are only three categories of time. There is the past, there is the present and there is the future. The past has conspired to make us who we are, but it cannot affect us going forward except to the extent that we allow it to do so. The past is a great learning tool, but it is only an indicator of the future if we allow it to be.

John Schaar, Professor Emeritus at the University of California, Santa Cruz, said it like this: 'The future is not a result of choices among alternative paths offered by the present, but a place that is created - created first in mind and will, created next in activity. The future is not some place we are going to, but one we are creating. The paths to it are not found but made, and the activity of making them changes both the maker and the destination.'

Unfortunately, the more we grow and learn the more we seem to limit our future. As small children everything seems possible but, as we pursue our education and our career, we seem to narrow instead of broadening the future outcomes we are willing to consider. If anything is possible, we must realise that everything is possible. Both the limitations and the pathways to success exist in our mind and imagination.

TIPS

1. The future belongs to people who see possibility.
2. The future belongs to those who believe in the beauty of their dreams.
3. The future is something which everyone reaches at the rate of 60 minutes an hour, whatever he/she does.
4. The future should be something we deserve, not something which is merely.
5. Write down short statements that remind you of what you're trying to change about the way you see the world. Put them in places where you'll see them every day, such as on your bathroom mirror. Some affirmations to start with are:

- Anything is possible.
- My circumstances do not create me. I create my circumstances.
- The only thing I can control is my attitude towards life.
- I always have a choice.
- I choose to live my positive side of life.

WHEN YOU FEEL THE HEAT

The most important aspect of taking responsibility for your life is to acknowledge that your life is your responsibility. No one can live your life for you. You are in charge. You felt the heat and realised you have to make a change.

TIPS

1. Stop waiting for other people to solve your problems for you. There are good reasons for this. First, in most cases they can't - not entirely. Other people may be able to change your immediate situation but they probably can't prevent difficulties from arising again, because then you find yourself in the same old position of needing to find someone willing to come and pick up the pieces again and the problem of dependence hasn't altered. Taking time to learn the skills you need to solve your own problems usually works much better in the long run and makes you much more popular, as people no longer avoid

you for fear of becoming over-involved in your problems. Remember - you are responsible.

Live as if you were to die tomorrow. Learn as if you were to live forever (Mahatma Gandhi).

Conclusion

In conclusion I have designed this book to be that navigator which will help you to get to your destination in any given endeavour. In life you are bound to get into a situation that makes you start, stop or move fast. Whichever trap you are in you will come out as long as you don't quit early.

Imagine driving your car or being driven on a journey. You're bound to approach some traffic lights that will make you stop the journey for a while: that will relate to the **struggle** or **experience** of life. You hit a kerb: that makes you feel like an **unsuccessful person.** You approach a zebra crossing and people are crossing: you need to hit the brake pedal and wait till everyone passes. While driving you need to be looking around for hazards or obstacles which might slow you down, so observation is vital: that will relate to **consistency.** You take the wrong turn: that makes you **embrace failure** and look for a **turning point.** You approach a crossroad and you need to stop, look left and look right before you proceed: that will relate to **opportunity.** Your fuel is about to run out and you need to go look for the nearest petrol station to fill up: that will relate to a **second chance.** Finally you are on your way to the motorway with no stopping until you reach your destination: that will relate to a **successful person** because on this whole journey there were some obstacles but you did not give up until you got to your destination, which is your goals.

You are one of a kind. You are lucky enough to have something that makes you different from everyone else. Embrace your individuality. One must know and trust that life is unique, unrepeatable, one of a kind, beautiful, simple, challenging, sweet, hard... and we just need to take a step back and find reasons to love it. Love your life, cherish it and never quit.

I've come to the **conclusion** that Mondays last 50 per cent longer than the other days (Turtle Dundee).

To succeed, jump as quickly at opportunities as you do at **conclusions** (Benjamin Franklin).

I've seen people spend days - if not months - researching and gathering data, but only at the end did they finally figure out what they were really looking for; then they have to redo a lot of stuff. If after a day or so you force yourself to put together your tentative **conclusions**, then you'll have guidance for the rest of your research (Robert Pozen).

I know people look at me and try to make **conclusions** about me immediately, based on the obvious, let's say (John Lone).

The ordinary patient goes to his doctor because he is in pain or some other discomfort and wants to be comfortable again; he is not in pursuit of the ideal of health in any direct sense. The doctor on the other hand wants to discover the pathological condition and control it if he can. The two are thus to some degree at cross purposes from the first, and unless the affair is brought to an early and happy **conclusion** this diversion of aims is likely to become more and more serious as the case goes on (Wilfred Trotter).

Architects cannot renovate it.
Businesses cannot incorporate it.
Developers cannot innovate it.
Engineers cannot calculate it.
Governments cannot legislate it.
Judges cannot adjudicate it.
Lawyers cannot litigate it.
Manufacturers cannot fabricate it.
Politicians cannot appropriate it.
Scientists cannot formulate it.
Technicians cannot generate it.
Only you can orchestrate it.

BE RELENTLESS...

Bibliography

Babauta, L (2009). *The Power of Less.*

Baron, R A (2004). *The Cognitive Perspective: A Valuable Tool for Answering Entrepreneurship's Basic 'Why' Questions.* Journal of Business Venturing. 19-221-239

Bragg, T (1997). *31 Days to High Self-Esteem.*

Buckminster, F (1982). *Critical Path.*

Douglas, M (2010). *How to Seize Life's Opportunities.*

Frankl, V E (2004). *Man's Search for Meaning*

www.goodreads.com

www.google.com

Hill, N (2007). *Think and Grow Rich.*

www.hilaryrettig.com

Mackay, H (2010). *What Makes Us Tick?*

Oxford English Dictionary (Second Edition, 1989).

Peters, T (2005). *Leadership, inspire, liberate, achieve.*

www.peterrussel.com

www.positivityblog.com

Schuller, R.H (2006). *Tough Times Never Last, But Tough People Do!*

www.sparkpeople.com

Tolle, E (2010). *The Power of Now: A Guide to Spiritual Enlightenment.*

www.wikipedia.org

ND - #0258 - 080726 - C0 - 216/138/9 - PB - 9781784560003 - Gloss Lamination